P9-CFU-669

The Life of a Cell

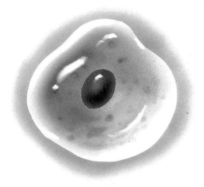

Andres Llamas Ruiz

Illustrations by Luis Rizo

Sterling Publishing Co., Inc.
New York

Illustrations by Luis Rizo
Text by Andrés Llamas Ruiz
Translated by Natalia Tizón

Library of Congress Cataloging-in-Publication Data

Llamas Ruiz, Andrés.
   [Celula. English]
   The life of a cell / by Andres Llamas Ruiz ; illustrations by Luis
Rizo.
         p.   cm. — (Cycles of life)
   Includes index.
   Summary: Describes the evolution of the first cell, cellular struc-
tures, and the processes by which cells reproduce and form
tissues.
   ISBN 0-8069-9741-9
   1. Cytology—Juvenile literature.   [1. Cells.]   I. Rizo, Luis, ill.
II. Title. III. Series: Llamas Ruiz, Andrés.   Secuencias de la
naturaleza.   English.
QH582.5.L5313   1997
574.87—dc21
                                                                    96–37952
                                                                        CIP
                                                                         AC

1   3   5   7   9   10   8   6   4   2

Published by Sterling Publishing Company, Inc.
387 Park Avenue South, New York, N.Y. 10016
Originally published in Spain by Ediciones Estes
©1996 by Ediciones Lema, S.L.
English version and translation © 1997 by Sterling Publishing Company, Inc.
Distributed in Canada by Sterling Publishing
% Canadian Manda Group, One Atlantic Avenue, Suite 105
Toronto, Ontario, Canada M6K 3E7
Distributed in Great Britain and Europe by Cassell PLC
Wellington House, 125 Strand, London WC2R 0BB, England
Distributed in Australia by Capricorn Link (Australia) Pty Ltd.
P.O. Box 6651, Baulkham Hills, Business Centre, NSW 2153, Australia
Printed and Bound in Spain
All rights reserved

Sterling ISBN 0-8069-9741-9

Table of Contents

Life appeared in the sea

The earth was "born" more than 4.5 billion years ago. Approximately 4 billion years ago, the elements that would ultimately create life began to develop in the warm seas that covered the earth. The first substances were hydrogen, water, ammonia, and methane. Millions of years later, under the influence of wind, sun, tides, and electrical charges, compounds rich in carbon gradually accumulated and spread all over the planet's surface. These were the first molecules!

Later on, these molecules grouped together to form semiliquid drops that were separated from the external environment by a protective coating. More than 3 billion years ago, these tiny pouch-shaped masses of jelly gradually evolved to form the first cells—the first and simplest forms of life capable of reproduction appeared. Life on earth was beginning.

1

2

3

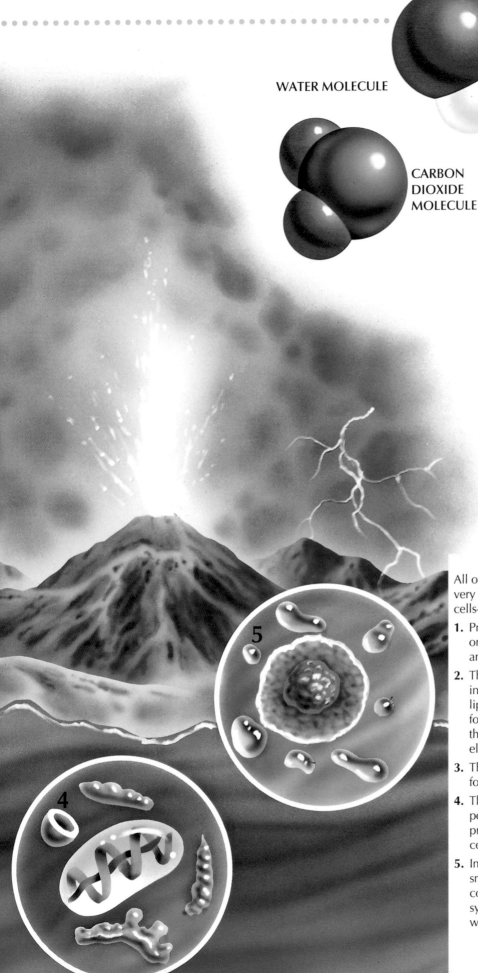

WATER MOLECULE

CARBON DIOXIDE MOLECULE

You can compare the appearance of molecules. As you can see, some of them, such as the cellulose molecule, are very complex. Only part of the cellulose molecule is shown in this illustration.

CELLULOSE MOLECULE

All organisms are formed from very simple elements called cells—the basic units of life.

1. Primitive oceans contained only hydrogen, water, ammonia, and methane.

2. Then, the first compounds rich in carbon (such as proteins, lipids, and carbohydrates) were formed under the influence of the wind, sun, tides, and electrical charges.

3. The first molecules grouped to form molecular compounds.

4. The first cells looked like tiny pouches surrounded by a protective membrane. These cells are called liposomes.

5. In the earth's primitive oceans, small, single-celled inhabitants consumed organic substances synthesized from hydrogen, water, ammonia, and methane.

The first cells were very simple

Each cell is a perfectly organized group of molecules capable of growing, responding to stimuli, moving, and reproducing. However, the first cells were very simple, since they had only a primary system of membranes and had not yet developed a nucleus separate from the rest of the cell. These types of cells were called "prokaryotes."

Prokaryotes are the simplest and most primitive cells. The best known of them are bacteria and blue-green algae. Prokaryotic cells are very small (only 0.000039 inches in length and diameter—a hundred times smaller than a pinhead) and their structure is very basic. On the outside, they are surrounded by a single cellular membrane, while inside there is a DNA molecule called the nucleoid, which contains genetic information.

Some prokaryotic cells have a special structure—the flagellum—on their surface, which allows them to move.

*Flagella (**a**), such as the one in this Euglena, are used to propel the cell and attract food particles by creating whirlwinds.*

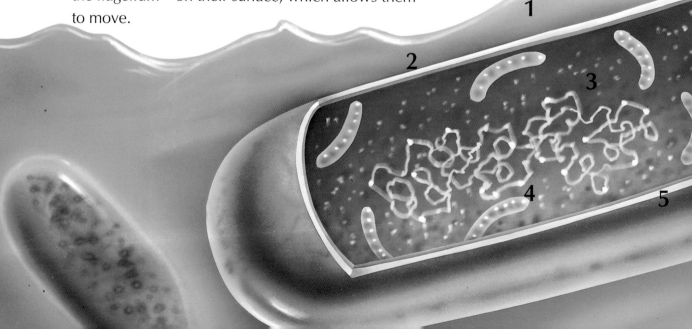

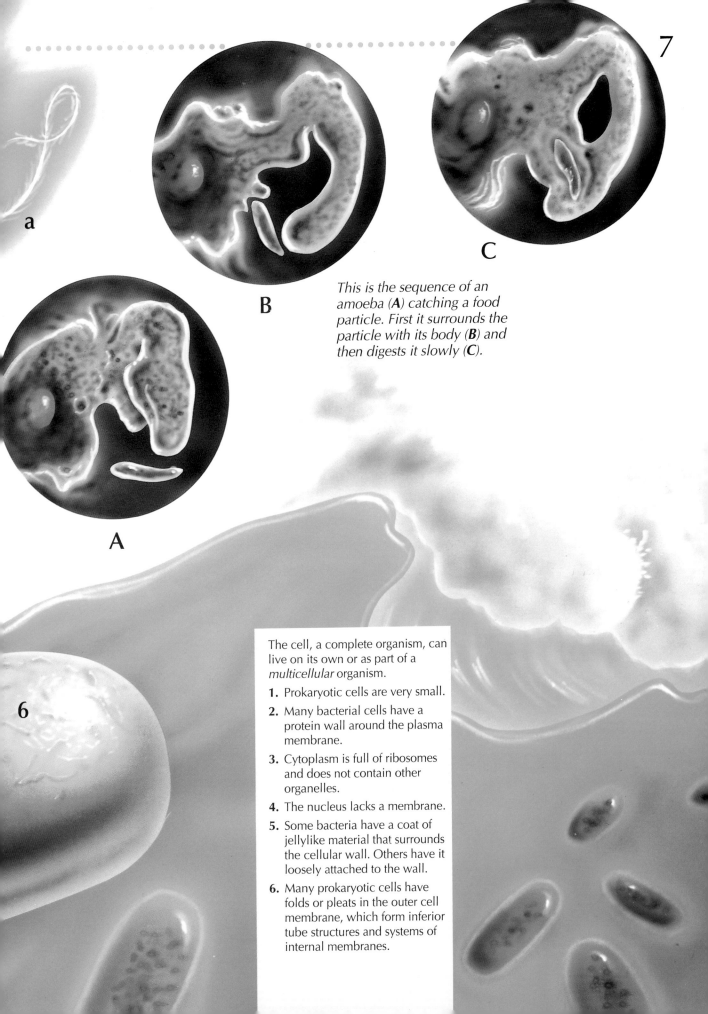

a

B

C

This is the sequence of an amoeba (A) catching a food particle. First it surrounds the particle with its body (B) and then digests it slowly (C).

A

6

The cell, a complete organism, can live on its own or as part of a *multicellular* organism.

1. Prokaryotic cells are very small.

2. Many bacterial cells have a protein wall around the plasma membrane.

3. Cytoplasm is full of ribosomes and does not contain other organelles.

4. The nucleus lacks a membrane.

5. Some bacteria have a coat of jellylike material that surrounds the cellular wall. Others have it loosely attached to the wall.

6. Many prokaryotic cells have folds or pleats in the outer cell membrane, which form inferior tube structures and systems of internal membranes.

The formation of a membrane

The cells adopted a sophisticated system of membranes that allowed them to obtain food, expel their waste, communicate with the outside world, divide, and so on. Each cell is surrounded by a very thin coating that controls the exchange of substances with the outside environment or with other cells.

But what is a membrane? The membrane is a very dynamic system formed by two layers of special pin-shaped molecules called *phospholipids*. Their heads search for the water while their tails avoid it. The parts that avoid the water are always on the inside of the membrane, while the hydrophilic heads (having affinity to the water) aim to the wet areas of the membrane. The membrane is so important that if it breaks, the cell dies immediately!

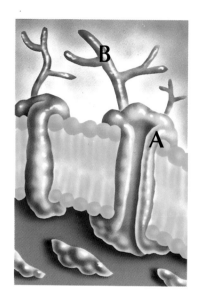

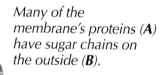

Many of the membrane's proteins (A) have sugar chains on the outside (B).

4

The membrane contains many proteins, some of which penetrate the double layer. These proteins transport substances vital to the cell that could not otherwise penetrate the membrane. Waste substances are also expelled by way of this path.

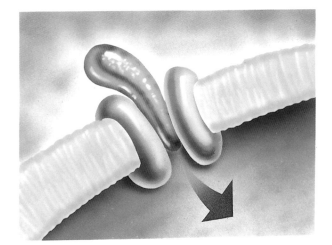

The larger the surface of the cell, the greater the exchange with the outside. Therefore, in order to increase their surface area, some cells (such as these of the intestines) have protrusions—cilia, pseudopods, or microvilli.

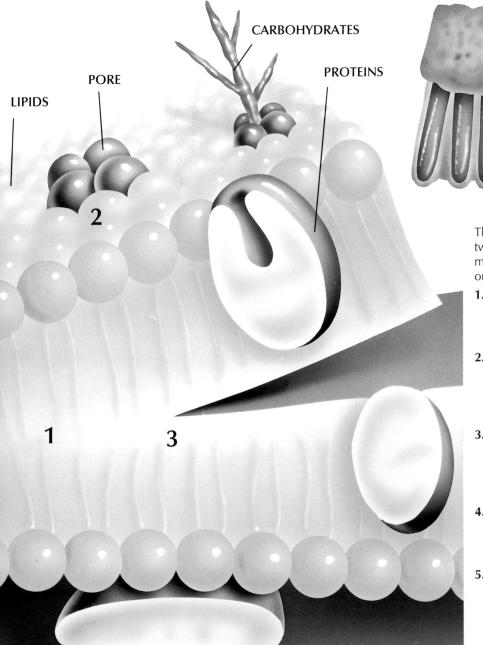

CARBOHYDRATES

PROTEINS

PORE

LIPIDS

2

1

3

The cytoplasmic membrane has two layers of lipids. These membranes are sometimes an inch or two thick.

1. Apart from protecting the cell, membranes control exchanges with the outside or with other cells.

2. The continuity of the plasma membrane allows vital molecules to penetrate the cell. It also allows the cell to adapt to changes in shape.

3. As a result, biological membranes can stretch, separate from, or join others without rupturing their membranes.

4. One side of the membrane is in contact with other cells or the environment, and the other side with the cytoplasm.

5. The cytoplasm is a sticky liquid within the membrane that contains reserve substances and organelles.

The first organisms with a nucleus were then formed

Many millions of years after the first prokaryotic organisms developed ("only" 1.5 billion years ago), eukaryotic cells—the first organism with a real cellular nucleus—appeared. This was a true "revolution," since these cells had a completely new structure. At first, they were also unicellular organisms, but gradually multicellular organisms appeared.

Eukaryotic cells are larger than prokaryotic cells; their volume can also be a hundred times greater.

Unlike prokaryotes, the cytoplasm of eukaryotic cells possesses a system of membranes and organelles surrounded by simple or double membranes. The organelles have very important functions, which allow eukaryotic cells to efficiently distribute their work.

In some tissues, such as skin, cells live very close to other cells of the same type. In some other cases, such as in blood cells, they do not.

The cell is the simplest and smallest form of life that can reproduce and use the environment to create new life. The nucleus of eukaryotic cells contains the hereditary information of the cell. The main difference between eukaryotic and prokaryotic cells is that the eukaryotic cell's nucleus has a membrane that separates it from the cytoplasm of the cell. Prokaryotic cells, on the other hand, have a nucleoid—not a nucleus—in which genetic information floats freely in the cell with no membrane to separate it.

1. The nucleus forms a great part of the total volume of the eukaryotic cell.

2. Organelles are abundant in the cytoplasm.

3. Organelles have important functions, such as breathing, secretion of substances, etc.

4. The best known organelles are the mitochondria (**a**), ribosomes (**b**), Golgi apparatus (**c**), and endoplasmic reticulum (**d**).

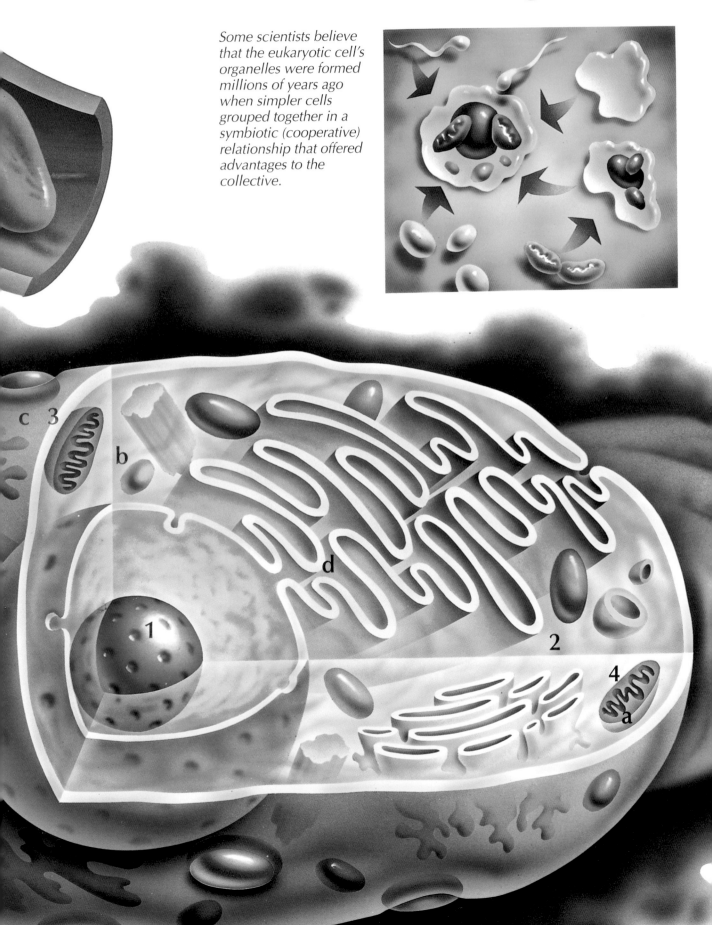

Some scientists believe that the eukaryotic cell's organelles were formed millions of years ago when simpler cells grouped together in a symbiotic (cooperative) relationship that offered advantages to the collective.

There is not only one model of cells, but many

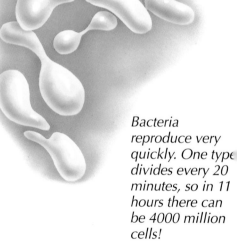

Acetabularia is an underwater green alga. It is formed by a single cell that can measure up to 3 inches in length!

Among animals, plants, and microorganisms, there are many kinds of cells that assume different shapes and perform different functions. The human body alone has hundreds of types of cells—each of them part of a specific organ or system (nervous system, muscles, blood, etc.). In fact, the more complex the organism, the more complex its cellular organization.

Some unicellular organisms, such as amoebas and paramecia, are totally independent and have complex organic structures. These organisms reproduce in different ways.

On the contrary, bacteria have a very simple organization. Even so, they have survived longer than any other organism and they are the most abundant cellular type on the planet. Some can live even in sulfur springs at higher temperatures than the boiling point.

Bacteria reproduce very quickly. One type divides every 20 minutes, so in 11 hours there can be 4000 million cells!

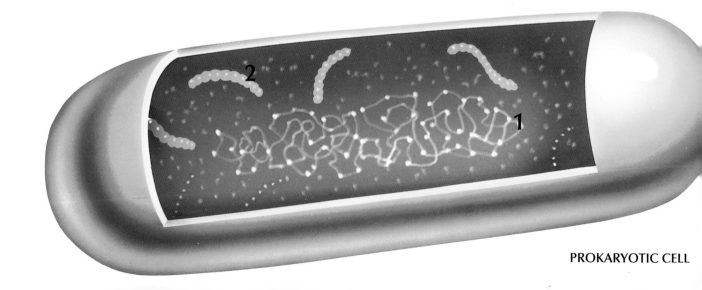

PROKARYOTIC CELL

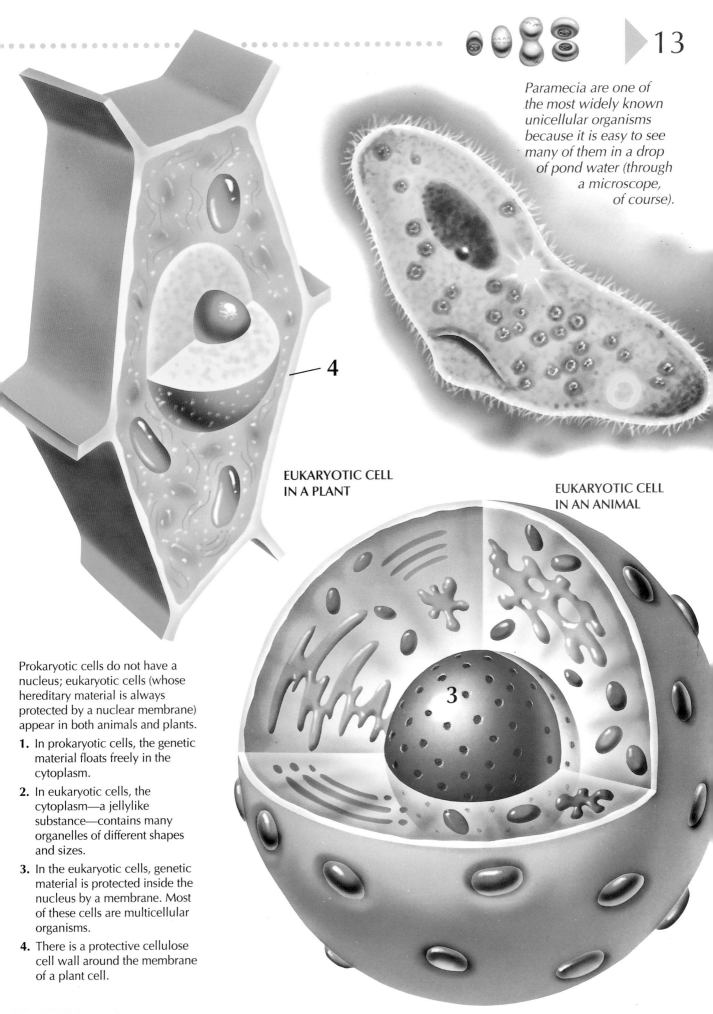

Paramecia are one of the most widely known unicellular organisms because it is easy to see many of them in a drop of pond water (through a microscope, of course).

EUKARYOTIC CELL IN A PLANT

— 4

EUKARYOTIC CELL IN AN ANIMAL

Prokaryotic cells do not have a nucleus; eukaryotic cells (whose hereditary material is always protected by a nuclear membrane) appear in both animals and plants.

1. In prokaryotic cells, the genetic material floats freely in the cytoplasm.

2. In eukaryotic cells, the cytoplasm—a jellylike substance—contains many organelles of different shapes and sizes.

3. In the eukaryotic cells, genetic material is protected inside the nucleus by a membrane. Most of these cells are multicellular organisms.

4. There is a protective cellulose cell wall around the membrane of a plant cell.

All cells need to find food

Life forms are comprised of many types of cells, although all of them—whether animal or plant—have common characteristics. For example, all cells need to obtain matter and energy so they can perform their vital activities, maintain their structure, and create new structures in order to grow. Cellular nutrition consists of a group of processes in which cells obtain substances from the outside and use them for their own functions. When the cell eats, small substances easily penetrate through the pores of the membrane by diffusion. If the particles are larger, they are absorbed through endocytosis or phagocytosis. In these cases, substances are trapped by an expansion of the cytoplasm membrane, which closes around them and pinches off to create a vesicle that penetrates the cell.

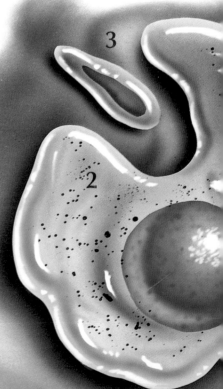

Phagocytosis is the normal way of eating for unicellular organisms such as protozoa. As you can see, they have many transport vesicles.

Phagocytosis is the absorption of solid particles by the cell surrounding them. This process is typical of the amoeba, the digestive cells of some invertebrates, and the white blood cells (leukocytes) of vertebrates. The difference between endocytosis and phagocytosis depends on the size of the particles caught.

1. During endocytosis, macromolecules and liquid drops are caught.
2. During phagocytosis, bigger particles are caught. Leukocytes, for example, ingest and destroy bacteria.
3. The cell approaches its "prey" and the membrane stretches to surround it.
4. The particle is then retained in a vesicle inside the cell.

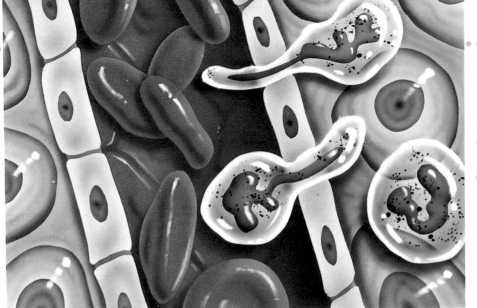

When there is an infection, leukocytes move quickly to "devour" invasive particles such as viruses.

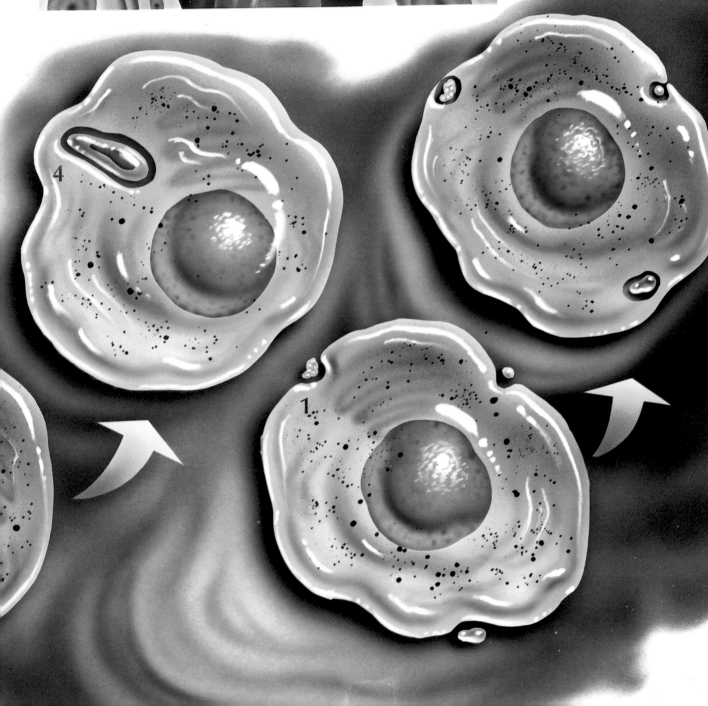

Then the cell digests its food

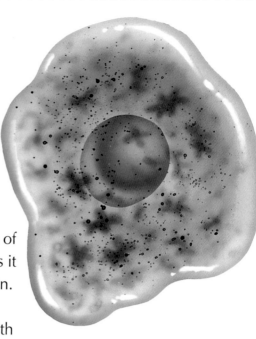

All cells obtain energy from the sun or the metabolism of combustible substances. After capturing the substances it needs, the cell digests them. Then the lysosomes step in. These are very special cellular organelles that contain digestive enzymes. Lysosomes fuse their membrane with the membrane of the vesicle containing the ingested particle and then add enzymes to break down the particle. Lysosomes are the real "stomach" of the cell, which digest the components of the particles that must be assimilated.

Lysosomes also help by destroying old organelles that need to be replaced. This process is called autophagy and consists of digesting some of the cellular elements, pieces of membrane, and aging cytoplasmic organelles. This is a controlled and necessary self-destructive process, since most cell organelles only live for several weeks.

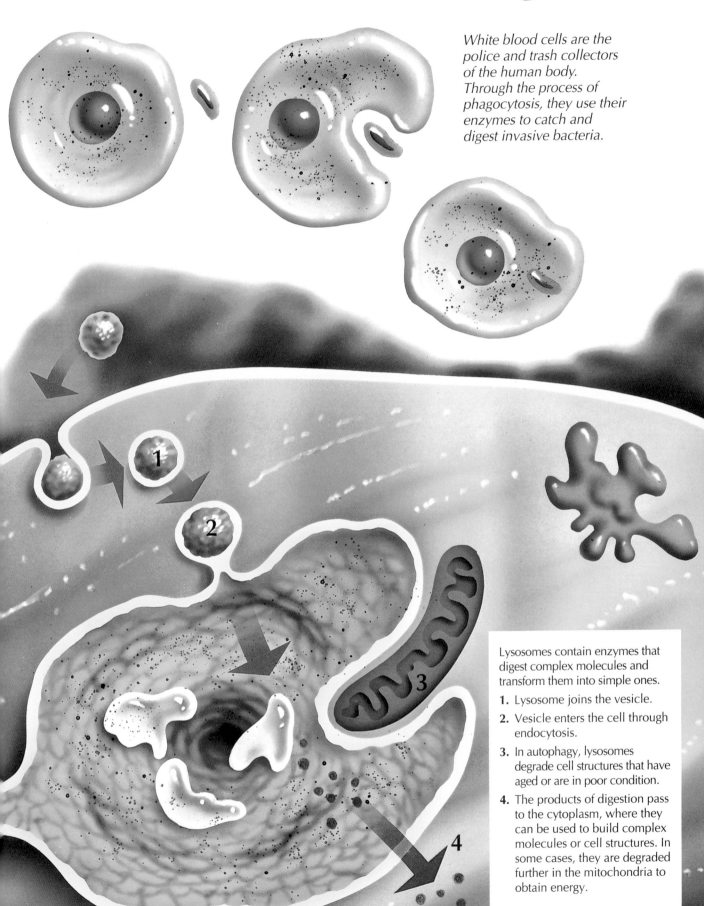

White blood cells are the police and trash collectors of the human body. Through the process of phagocytosis, they use their enzymes to catch and digest invasive bacteria.

Lysosomes contain enzymes that digest complex molecules and transform them into simple ones.

1. Lysosome joins the vesicle.

2. Vesicle enters the cell through endocytosis.

3. In autophagy, lysosomes degrade cell structures that have aged or are in poor condition.

4. The products of digestion pass to the cytoplasm, where they can be used to build complex molecules or cell structures. In some cases, they are degraded further in the mitochondria to obtain energy.

Cells "breathe" through the mitochondria

Inside the eukaryotic cells are very special organelles, the mitochondria, which are the real "power plants" of the cells. The mitochondria convert chemical energy in the food (such as carbohydrates) into the energy that is necessary for the cells' vital processes. Then, this energy is also used to build molecules that drive a variety of cellular reactions.

What is a mitochondrion? It is an organelle encased within two membranes. The outer one is smooth and permeable to many small molecules. The inner one is less permeable and wrinkles by forming pleats or folds in which energy synthesis takes place. These folds are abundant in cells that require a great deal of energy, such as muscle cells.

Mitochondria multiply by division. From one mitochondrion, two new ones appear.

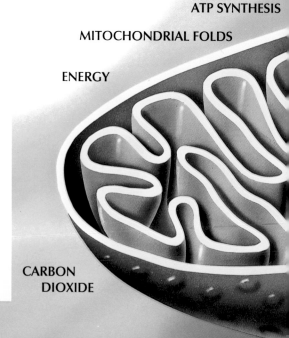

ATP SYNTHESIS

MITOCHONDRIAL FOLDS

ENERGY

CARBON DIOXIDE

Inside the mitochondrion, the energy needed by the eukaryotic cell is produced.

1. The shape of the mitochondrion varies. It may be rod-shaped, oval-shaped, or round.

2. Its numbers can also vary, from ten or twenty in microorganisms to more than one thousand in muscle cells.

3. Membranes are separated by the intermembrane space.

4. The mitochondrion works using atmospheric oxygen; this is why it is located close to the source of oxygen, in the cytoplasm.

5. Apart from energy, the mitochondrion also produces small amounts of carbon dioxide and water.

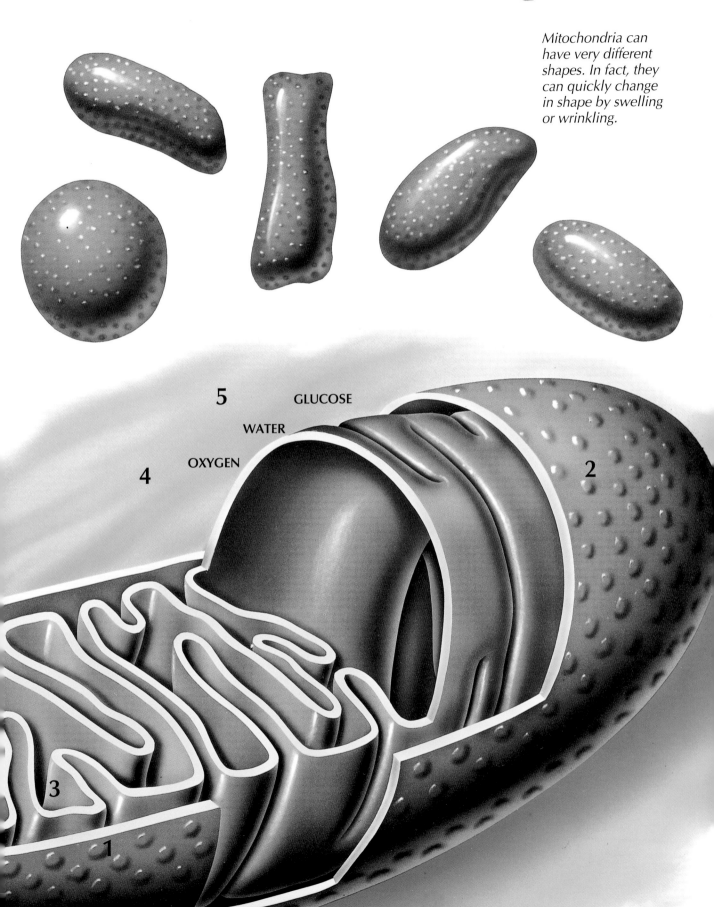

Mitochondria can have very different shapes. In fact, they can quickly change in shape by swelling or wrinkling.

5

GLUCOSE

WATER

OXYGEN

4

2

3

1

The nucleus is the most important part of a eukaryotic cell

The nucleus is a voluminous sphere at the center of the eukaryotic cell. Plant and animal cells are eukaryotic cells, which means that the nucleus is isolated from the cytoplasm by a membrane called the nuclear membrane.

Inside the nucleus are the most complex organic molecules: the *nucleic acids*. These are formed by "chains" of smaller molecules called nucleotides, which are made up of sugars, nitrogen, and phosphates.

There are two types of nucleic acids, the deoxyribonucleic acid (DNA) and the ribonucleic acid (RNA). RNA takes part in the synthesis of the proteins. The DNA, however, is responsible for transmitting hereditary characteristics from one generation to the next!

DNA molecules have a very particular shape—a double helix formed by two complementary chains that contain nucleotides curled parallel to each other to resemble a spiral staircase. DNA is tightly curled onto itself. If it were completely stretched out, the DNA of a human cell would measure more than 6.5 feet.

In the nuclear membrane, there are pores that allow for the passage of some substances and special molecules.

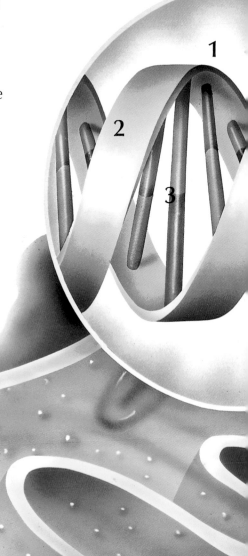

The DNA inside the nucleus contains all genetic or hereditary information passed from generation to generation, including hair color, eye color, etc. In fact, DNA molecules are like an "instruction manual" to assemble new cells identical to the mother cell.

1. Each DNA molecule is formed by two chains braided in the shape of a double helix.

2. Each chain is formed by the repetition of a molecule called the nucleotide.

3. The links between the pairs of nucleotides keep both chains connected.

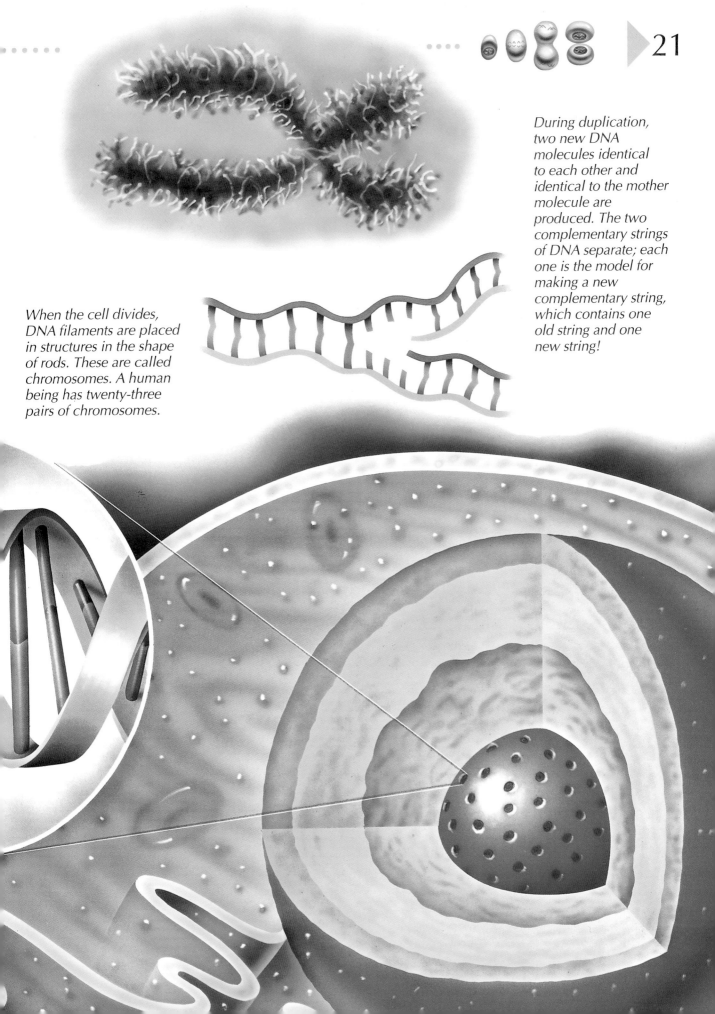

During duplication, two new DNA molecules identical to each other and identical to the mother molecule are produced. The two complementary strings of DNA separate; each one is the model for making a new complementary string, which contains one old string and one new string!

When the cell divides, DNA filaments are placed in structures in the shape of rods. These are called chromosomes. A human being has twenty-three pairs of chromosomes.

The cell needs to reproduce

In order to survive, cells must reproduce. This can happen in two different ways. The most simple and primitive way of division is mitosis, in which the mother cell divides into two identical cells. Unicellular organisms such as bacteria and protozoa reproduce this way.

The other way of reproducing is meiosis. This process uses sexual cells called spermatozoids and eggs. When the first organisms with a nucleus appeared (more than a billion years ago), the conditions necessary for this type of "sexual" reproduction were created. This was one of the most important events in nature. Using this form of reproduction, individual inheritances of genetic information are mixed over generations to form new combinations where only the most well adapted survive. This is the basis of evolution!

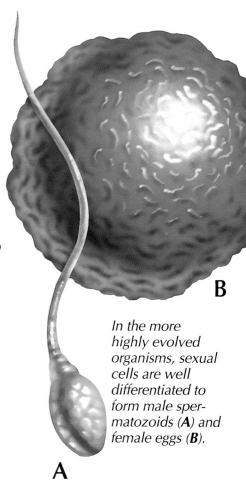

*In the more highly evolved organisms, sexual cells are well differentiated to form male spermatozoids (**A**) and female eggs (**B**).*

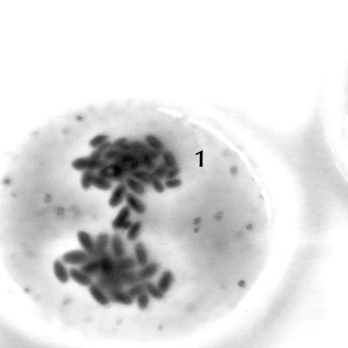

 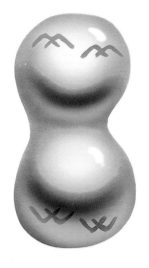 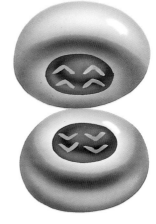

In multicellular organisms, mitosis replaces dead cells with new ones. The cells have a short life. A human intestine cell, for example, lives for only 3 to 5 days.

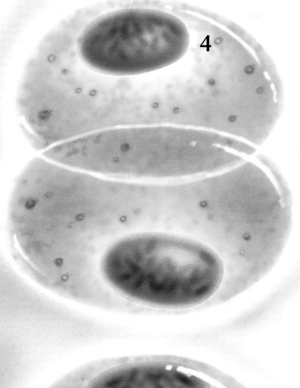

4

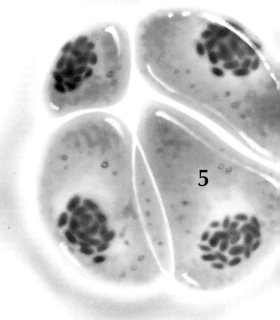

5

3

During meiosis, instead of a simple bipartition of the cell nucleus (mitosis), the chromosomes of the cell divide and split into two new cells.

1. Homologous chromosomes separate.
2. They are distributed into two new nuclei.
3. Each new cell receives one simple set of chromosomes.
4. The cytoplasm of the two new cells begins to separate.
5. In multicellular organisms, the fertilized egg will divide again and again to form a new organism with millions of cells.

Inside the cell, there are many more membranes

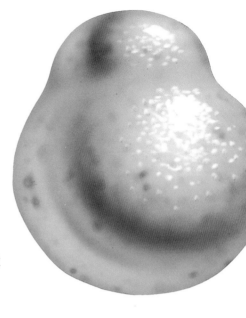

Apart from the nuclear membrane, all eukaryotic cells have a huge network of internal membranes that carry out vital functions. For example, some isolate energy centers (chloroplasts that are present in plant cells and protozoa only, and mitochondria) from the rest of the cell.

The endoplasmic reticulum is a continuous network of cavities connected among themselves. It is responsible for the synthesis and secretion of protein and lipids (fats). This endoplasmic reticulum surrounds the nucleus (where it forms the nuclear membrane) and faces the cytoplasm (where it communicates with the system of membranes of the Golgi apparatus).

The Golgi apparatus is formed by a pile of pouches in the shape of a disk surrounded by small vesicles. Its job is to sort the proteins and lipids and send them off to the appropriate places.

Ribosomes

Ribosomes are spherical particles that swim freely through the cytoplasm or stick to the walls of the endoplasmic reticulum. They normally gather to synthesize proteins.

GOLGI APPARATUS

4

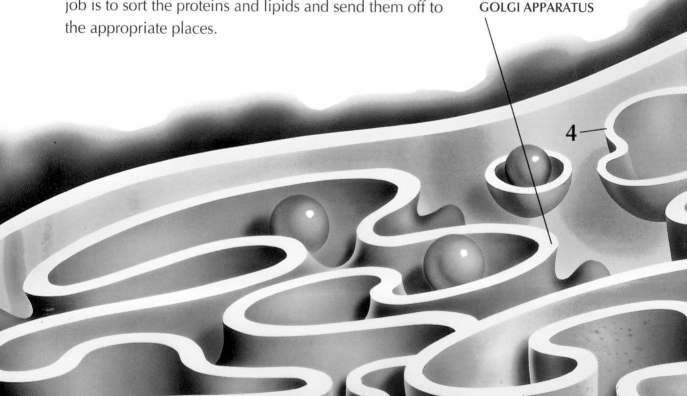

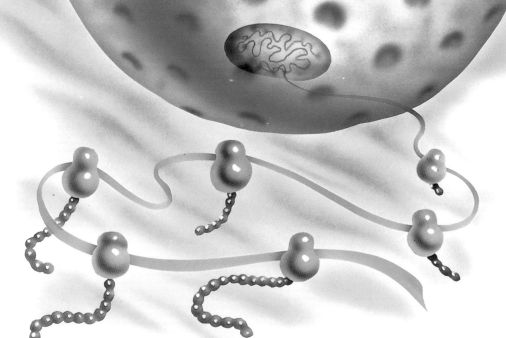

The synthesis of proteins

Inside the nucleus, DNA transcribes into RNA. Then, the RNA emerges from the nucleus through the pores and moves into the ribosomes to form proteins. The ribosomes are the protein factories!

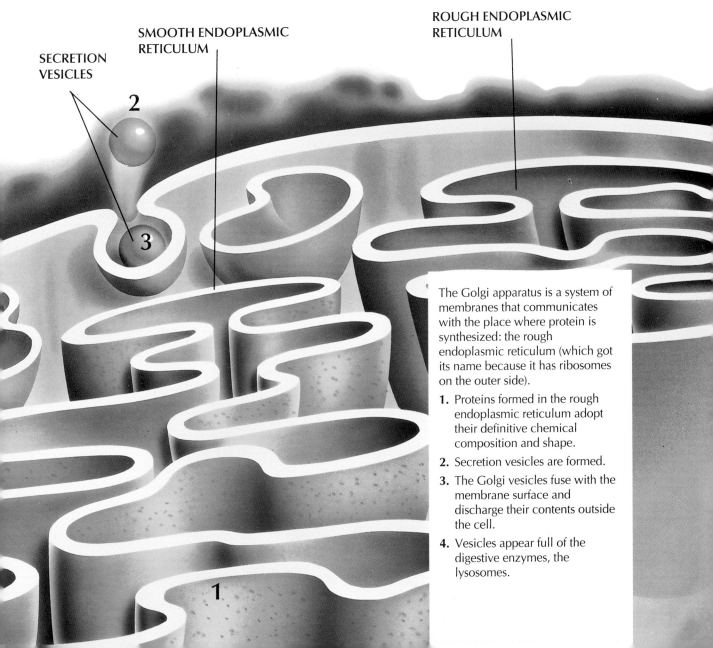

SECRETION VESICLES

SMOOTH ENDOPLASMIC RETICULUM

ROUGH ENDOPLASMIC RETICULUM

The Golgi apparatus is a system of membranes that communicates with the place where protein is synthesized: the rough endoplasmic reticulum (which got its name because it has ribosomes on the outer side).

1. Proteins formed in the rough endoplasmic reticulum adopt their definitive chemical composition and shape.

2. Secretion vesicles are formed.

3. The Golgi vesicles fuse with the membrane surface and discharge their contents outside the cell.

4. Vesicles appear full of the digestive enzymes, the lysosomes.

Plant cells differentiate themselves from animal cells

About 2.3 billion years ago, cyano-bacteria (or blue-green algae) appeared. These organisms were very successful and reproduced very fast because they were capable of something completely new—*photosynthesis*.

A few million years later, cells perfected an organelle called the chloroplast, which was capable of using energy directly from the sun. The first cells with chloroplasts were green algae called phytoplankton.

Photosynthesis occurs in the membranes of the chloroplasts, due to their color components (chlorophyll and carotene). These pigment molecules allow plants to absorb sunlight.

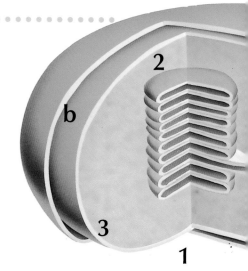

Plastids are organelles that exist in all plant cells. The ones that contain the chlorophyll pigment are called chloroplasts.

The chloroplast is the place where the plant cell performs photosynthesis. The number of chloroplasts varies from one cell to another. For example, the photosynthetic algae only have one or two, whereas the cells of more evolved plants contain several hundred.

1. The chloroplast is surrounded by two membranes, the external plastidial membrane (**a**) and the internal plastidial membrane (**b**).

2. The thylakoid membrane is a specialized membrane in the chloroplast where the light-dependent reactions of photosynthesis take place.

3. Associated with the internal membranes of chloroplasts is a group of pigments responsible for absorbing light.

4. Plastids have their own genetic material (a DNA molecule independent from the one in the nucleus).

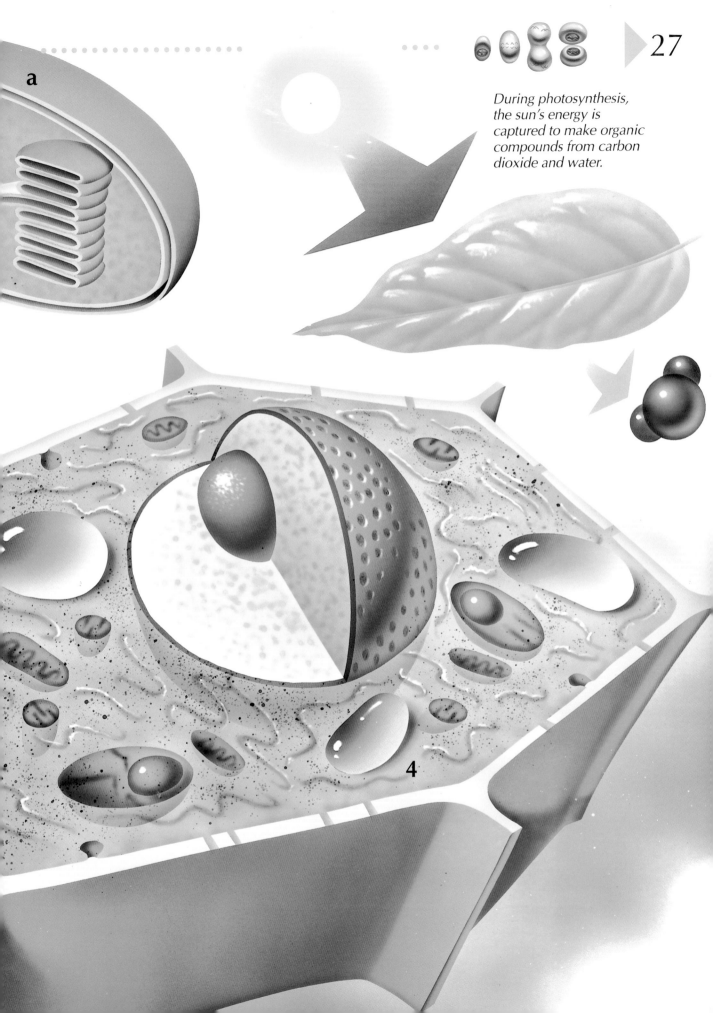

a

During photosynthesis, the sun's energy is captured to make organic compounds from carbon dioxide and water.

4

The cell relates to the world around it

Cells do not live isolated from the outside world; they constantly receive information about the environment. In order to receive this information, they have a "cellular sensibility" that can detect chemical, physical, electric, and thermal stimuli. When certain changes are detected, the cell responds in order to survive. The membrane plays a very important role in these processes, since it has many recognition structures and it is also a selective barrier for substances entering the cell.

   The cell responds to stimuli in many different ways. Some cells can move. For example, when there is an infection in the body, chemical substances are released, attracting white cells to the infected areas!

Despite their thick cellulose wall, plant cells exchange substances through perforations called pits.

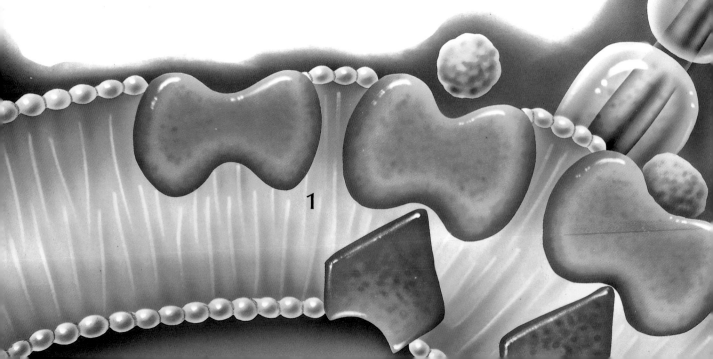

1

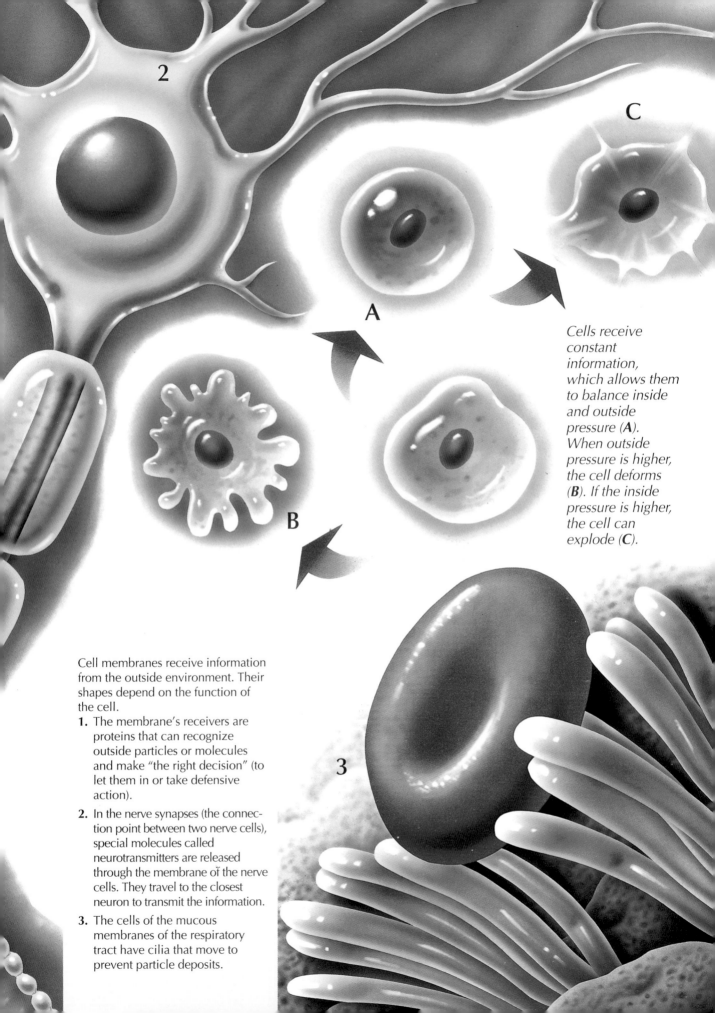

2

C

A

Cells receive constant information, which allows them to balance inside and outside pressure (A). When outside pressure is higher, the cell deforms (B). If the inside pressure is higher, the cell can explode (C).

B

3

Cell membranes receive information from the outside environment. Their shapes depend on the function of the cell.

1. The membrane's receivers are proteins that can recognize outside particles or molecules and make "the right decision" (to let them in or take defensive action).

2. In the nerve synapses (the connection point between two nerve cells), special molecules called neurotransmitters are released through the membrane of the nerve cells. They travel to the closest neuron to transmit the information.

3. The cells of the mucous membranes of the respiratory tract have cilia that move to prevent particle deposits.

Cells gather to form tissues and each type of cell adopts a specialty

How is a multicellular organism formed? In multicellular organisms, all cells come from the divisions of only one cell, called a zygote, that is formed by the union of two sexual cells during fertilization. However, not all cells are similar. Actually, they are very different from one another (in size, shape, number, etc.). In multicellular organisms, each cell is specialized for specific tasks, which is a much more efficient way than if all cells were required to do everything.

A tissue consists of a group of cells with common morphological characteristics (size, shape, etc.) that perform the same function—for example, the bone, muscular, nervous tissues, etc. Then, the tissues gather to form organs, such as the lungs, heart, etc.

Muscle-tissue cells quickly contract and relax. This is how they provide the body's locomotion and movement.

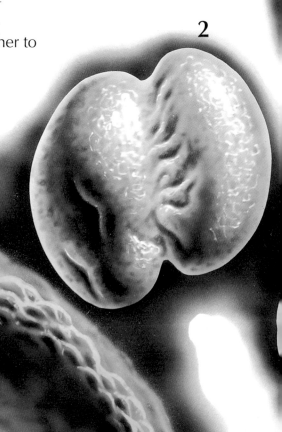

1

2

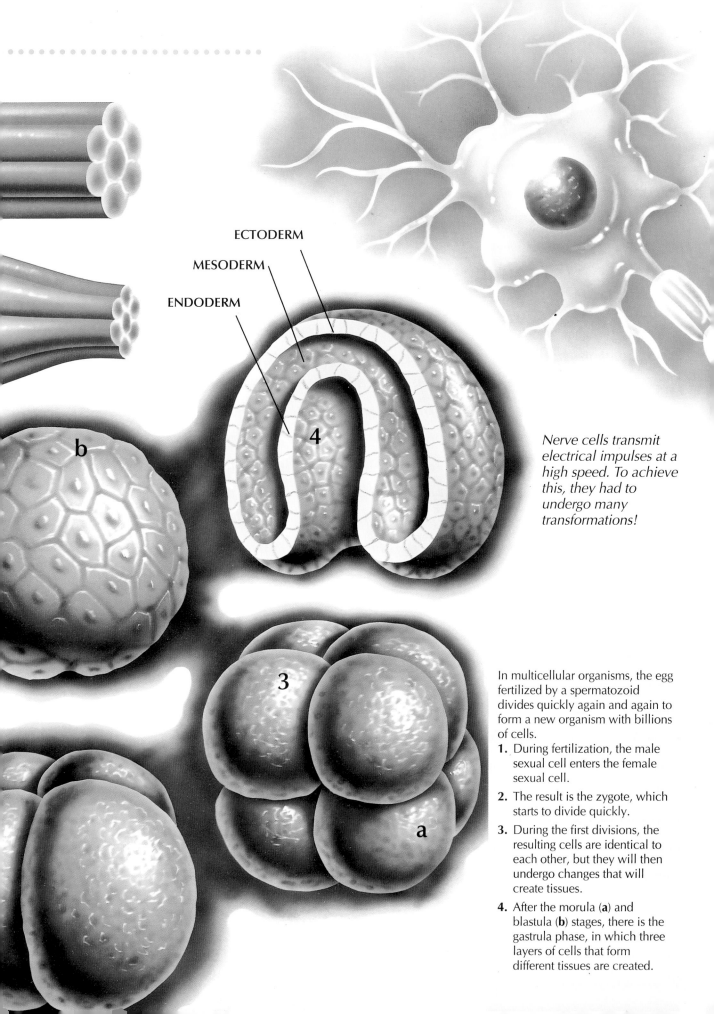

ECTODERM

MESODERM

ENDODERM

4

b

3

a

Nerve cells transmit electrical impulses at a high speed. To achieve this, they had to undergo many transformations!

In multicellular organisms, the egg fertilized by a spermatozoid divides quickly again and again to form a new organism with billions of cells.

1. During fertilization, the male sexual cell enters the female sexual cell.

2. The result is the zygote, which starts to divide quickly.

3. During the first divisions, the resulting cells are identical to each other, but they will then undergo changes that will create tissues.

4. After the morula (a) and blastula (b) stages, there is the gastrula phase, in which three layers of cells that form different tissues are created.

Glossary

ATP: A key compound that is formed by the breaking down of food molecules to supply the energy for many biochemical cellular processes.

Bacteria: Unicellular microorganisms that can be of many different kinds. Some are useful for agriculture, some cause diseases, some others take part in fermentation and the breaking down of dead animals and plants.

Carotene: A yellow pigment that can be found in carrots and other yellow food.

Chlorophyll: Green pigment that can be found in the leaves and tender stems of plants and is fundamental for photosynthesis.

Diffusion: The movement of molecules or ions from places in which they are abundant to those where their concentration is lower. This is a very simple type of movement useful for very short distances.

DNA: Abbreviation for deoxyribonucleic acid, which is a molecule containing the hereditary information of the organism.

Enzymes: Proteins that break down organic compounds to help with digestion.

Fertilization: The moment when a spermatozoid enters an egg, beginning the development of an embryo.

Glucose: Carbohydrate found in animal and plant tissues.

Hydrophilic: That which can be easily absorbed by water and have affinity with it.

Metabolism: Chemical and physical processes by which organisms extract and transform energy from their environment.

Molecule: Group of atoms that are the smallest size of a pure substance and that can be free of the substance without losing its properties.

Multicellular: Organism formed by more than one cell, in which the work is specialized for certain types of cells.

Nucleic acids: They are the DNA and the RNA. They are very important for the transmission of genetic information and protein synthesis.

Organelles: Cell organs that perform a precise function, such as mitochondria or chloroplasts.

Phagocytosis: Absorption of solid particles by the cell, in which a cell membrane surrounds a particle and brings it into the cell. This is characteristic of amoebas, the digestive cells of some invertebrates, and the white blood cells of the vertebrate.

Phospholipid: Type of fatty compound which contains phosphoric acids and which can be found in the membranes of animals and plants.

Photosynthesis: Process by which green plants synthesize organic matter from carbon dioxide through using light as a source of energy.

Vesicles: Small pouches or spheres surrounded by a membrane inside the cytoplasm of the cell, in which various substances can be transported or stored.

Zygote: The cell resulting from the union of two sexual cells (one masculine and one feminine).

Index

Audubon Regional -- Jackson Br.
JNF   X 574.87   C3
Llamas Ruiz,   The life of a cell.

3 0086 0001 8509 3

X574.87 Llamas Ruiz, Andres
         The life of a cell.

                            10/98

No AR Test   JACKSON BRANCH
Available

Audubon Regional Library
Clinton, Louisiana

                                        DEMCO